## Sarah Jackson

*With best wishes,*
*Sarah*

Milk
© Sarah Jackson 2008

Illustration © Paul Radburn 2008

All rights reserved. No part of this pamphlet may be reproduced, stored in a retrieval system, or transmitted in any form, or by any means, electronic or otherwise, without the prior written permission of Pighog Press.

Sarah Jackson has asserted her right to be identified as the author of this work in accordance with the Copyright, Designs and Patents Act 1998.

First published December 2008 by

**pighog**

PO Box 145
Brighton BN1 6YU
UK

info@pighog.co.uk
www.pighog.co.uk

In association with THE SOUTH
www.thesouth.org.uk

ISBN 978-1-906309-07-7

Design by Curious
www.curiouslondon.com

**Contents**

| | |
|---|---|
| Two Mothers | 5 |
| What Daddy Built | 6 |
| Vanishing Twin | 7 |
| Touch Papers | 8 |
| Pig | 9 |
| Tender | 10 |
| Night Fishing | 11 |
| Aristotle's Lantern | 12 |
| Leftovers | 13 |
| Like a Smile | 14 |
| Revolution | 15 |
| Friday 12.03 | 16 |
| A Quarter To | 17 |
| The Instant of my Death | 18 |
| Holy Cow | 19 |
| Momos and Tea | 20 |
| Childish Things | 21 |
| The Yard | 22 |
| November | 23 |
| Clam | 24 |
| Footing | 25 |
| Turn out the light | 26 |

For my mum, with love and thanks

**Two Mothers**

One just crawled into my cot,
laid her head in my lap,
I'm tired, she said.
I stroke gin caked lips,
sweep away the hair that cracks her cheek.
Her old eyes close;
I smile, hold onto her head,
gather her to me
as dark walks past the window.

I have another mother below
who is cleaning walls, singing,
her tight, white hips spinning,
while this one sleeps.

Too big for my bed
she's a coal sack leaking milk,
skirts mashed between slumped legs,
hands huge, wider than my face.

Her arm falls out of the cot,
too fat to fold back. She won't wake
and though toothless I bite her.
I don't mean to make her cry.

There's not room for us both,
and cold, hairless, hungry
I slip through the bars easily.
Though I have two mothers
neither hears me climb in
with the boneless dolls,
close the toy-box lid.

**What Daddy Built**

That night the dogs cried again and woke you.
Wanting to be still-small you climbed inside the doll's house
that daddy built. Sunk below your bed line, it waited, floored.

In the darkness your bed was a long, hard road
and you belly-crawled on all fours as if you were still a baby.
Hem rucked around your gut, you were naked under a pale purple nightie,

your bare bum smiling up at the moon as you crept;
your big-girl body a white worm, big-girl skin rubbing nylon;
static cracking up the dark with tiny forks of yellow,

like yellow boned fingers with long yellow nails
and where your big-girl bed fell away steeply you dropped to the floor.
The dogs cried again and blind, you reached out, found the house

that daddy built. You stroked its door, finger-felt its floor,
placed your cheek on glossy gables. You ran your tongue-tip
all up the walls; bit down, the wood splinters sweet, cool.

You licked the shiny red roof and it was so slick it slid nearly
deep inside you. Truly, you could eat this doll's house that daddy built,
or it could eat you. And then you unhooked the door, reached inside

to touch the doll people, the length of your white arm
folding right into its hot, red belly. Finally you slept,
your head in the kitchen window, a daddy doll in your teeth.

**Vanishing Twin**

For years, I've hid
in a cracked hotel
tipping the moors:

I sleep days, among piles
and piles of laundry;
nights, I steal dreams

wrap them up
in soft white towels
longing for you

my duck egg girl
my vanishing twin.
Do you remember me?

I still feel the ache
of your lidless space
your imprint on my skin.

**Touch Papers**

It is white when I wake
so I wear my old navy dufflecoat,
finding them in my pocket
tucked inside a brown envelope.

Here she is. Squatting,
she is the callous
on her size seven heel,
fingers tinsel chipped

from schoolboard chalk,
driftwood nails, thumb
a pummelstone mouse
smiling my cheek.

Here he is. Flat out,
he is the lip of his ear
swan soft, dust flecked,
the sound of a dog pawing.

He has grey whiskers that beat
like hair on coral
and his eyelid when he blinks
is deep, pooling, purple.

I hold them inside my pocket
fondle skin letters
climbing the library steps.
They barely make a sound

a rustle, a peep, as I slip
them between the pages
of a dictionary, under
Mother, Father.

**Pig**

When people ask
who I think I am
I tell them I grew up
with pigs. I ate
off their fat bellies
slept against their
hairy snouts.
I say all that
as if it explains
things. I'm lying.

There's been no pigs
for years: just horses
and some corn.
But when I think
about who I am
or where I'm from
I still see the shape
of their trotters
still feel their solid
hoary skins.

**Tender**

Back wheel jammed,
I shimmy up the aisle, groaning.
A black-eyed baby is watching,
squatting in my trolley.
I stare back,
rest a bag of red grapes by its left thigh,
hand pick twelve Royal Gala to place by its right.
Fling in oyster mushrooms, so plump
they bleed,
and three loaves of white sliced,
soft innards like the baby's face, doughy.
I like tins; the clunk when they drop,
their palm weight, the way they dent,
squashing the bananas
and the baby.
I swap my handbag for a frozen chicken,
buy all the cheddar they've got,
cram it in
and sashay over to the fish.

Finally, loaded,
I rest a single skinned salmon steak
on the baby's face,
skip towards the checkout,
singing.

**Night Fishing**

My father sails a boat curved like a cradle,
paints eyes on the bow to ward off evil,
mends sails with Grandma's wedding dress.
The mast is polished oak: tall, dead-straight –
the barrel of a shotgun. Splitting
the estuary into open waters, the hull
glistens with sea-bream, beautiful fat cod.

I sleep right here, in the brown cardboard box
stowed beneath his tiller. I am small, snug,
the tip and roll of waves runs through my marrow.
Every night, I wait for my father to tidy his nets,
part his legs and look down at me, lying upturned
like a little trout, my belly slick with sea salt.
Hello shrimp, he says, then tells me about my mother:

She had a thin smile like the fold of a fish-fin,
a wetness that gathered between her back-teeth,
and sometimes, during long, clear nights,
fishermen still see the length of her arms,
her open face, as she offers herself to the gods;
her back strapped to a polished oak mast,
her arms fastened to sails of white lace.

**Aristotle's Lantern**

You are a sea-urchin, legless,
as you slide along the blue-rimmed
pool-side to the shallow-end
where I'm untangling my goggles.
Ducking up and under, your white cap
is a beacon; when you smile
I see your small hollow teeth.

I tell you I've had this awful cold
for weeks; that's why I haven't called
for quite some time. You won't listen:
*Really Mother,* you say,
pulling yourself out of the water,
removing your swimming cap.
You have dyed your hair brown again.

I hug you back – all arms and legs –
try to pretend we are not naked
but for the blue and black lycra
strapped to our backsides, our chests.
I notice my knuckles,
yellow and globby like fungi,
clutching the silver steps.

When you kiss me again I look away,
watch water-ants run down my skin.
You touch my hand: *What is it, Mother?*
Only I cannot say that when you move in
to kiss me, you drip water on my face
as if from a rice spoon, and I'm afraid
I might bite your tongue if we speak.

**Leftovers**

The second Saturday of every month
they remind me how to work the remote,
point out the rocket salad with walnut and blue cheese,
kindly suggesting I don't touch
the thermostat or the baby.
Then they go to friends' for dinner
or to that nice little Thai place on the corner
of Bridge Street, just the two of them.

Watching Casualty on wide-screen
I thumb through last year's holiday snaps,
left out under the solicitor's letter.
I side-step the salad but sip sauvignon blanc
from an open bottle,
eat Cheerios out of the packet,
fat fingers greasy with spit.
At a quarter to, I check the baby
is breathing.
Watching him feels like spying
and I sit on stripped pine floors,
pretending it's all mine.

They rattle the keys as a warning.
Warmed by wine she offers me a drink,
insists I stay.
We can have a proper chat over breakfast, she says.
Yes, she says, as she always does, do stay.
In the spare room, I undress, wait,
listen for the sounds of them breathing.

Night hums softly,
and by dawn my legs are wound around
the white silk of her wedding gown.

**Like a Smile**

Mother in a yellow
sweater turns blue
then black beneath
the climbing frame
weaver ants pouring
out of her nose
but I don't

Breaking a beer bottle
on the toilet bowl
I finger the lovely slab
of slippery green
test the sharp lilt
on the inside of my
pink and white

Wearing my cut
like a smile I visit
mother in her yellow
sweater – come here
she says – I haven't
given you a proper
hello yet

**Revolution**

We revolt at night, unzipping our red silk skins
turning the pearly ridges of our backs on the moon
white knuckles hovering in a hall of black tulips
there are hoards of us, and I'm in charge of the bones

we slither on our limp bellies down to the crocus fields
the touch of our bald body-tips making the grass roots sing
if they see us coming, they'll beat us with feathers again
we revolt at night, unzipping our red silk skins

the old birds live in the flowers, with huge rotten wings
but shorter than grass, we quiver on down and through
nosing in nests tucked inside the damp dark soil
turning the pearly ridges of our backs on the moon

I haven't eaten for years, and I am starving hungry
oh, listen – I tell you, I haven't eaten for years
so I strangle the blackbird and dig out its bones
white knuckles hovering in a hall of black tulips

there are cracked up pieces of the moon swimming in here
then a wing bone reaches out of the birthday-blue to gag me
it is quite sharp, could easily slit my slack-skin throat
only there are hoards of us, and I'm in charge of the bones.

**Friday 12.03**

You and I will meet
unexpectedly outside
the glass library
on Jubilee Street
and we will smile
shyly as the clock
inches forward to 04;
then we will blink
and feel it catch
in our lashes.

Around us the toddler
the builder, the tramp
will feel it too:
these small soft beads
of white settle
on our hair, our cheeks
and in that second
we will look up
only it won't be snow
nor dust, nor light

but something else
entirely: something
our mothers never
taught us; a feeling
we can neither know
nor name; a deep settling
that will frighten us
yet make us smile
at each other
all the same.

**A Quarter To**

The grass is damp and my tights
still flat out on the peach carpet, so I tell you

Hurry. We're early you say, but you know nothing
about nothing. Still, your tongue glints

as we step out into the night.
Twist the bottle, not the cork, I say. Quick –

and you bellow when it shoots up
into the moon's open mouth.

We swallow but the moon spits it back out
and as the cork lands by my feet

I see you peek at my butter toes,
remember earlier, how you'd smiled at my tights –

thick, woollen – you plucking bobbles
from behind my thighs. To distract you now

I tell you about my pancake baby:
Oh, you know nothing;

she is near see-through and her eyes
are cats-eyes yes and her face is fish-skin

and her mouth is her lips is her hips.
Yes, round and snug, a pancake baby,

pockets of peaches, pillows of cream,
and when she cries, I tell you, she leaks poppy seeds.

**The Instant of My Death**

The bus was crammed and the fat man rubbed against my leg like a damp cat
while you read The Jatarka Tales three rows from the back

and we all stumbled on; wheels and hours grinding, tripping
as Spiti rose up around us, sky propped open by its peaks.

I traced the rockline on the window with my finger,
counted cows and gompas, felt my eyes glaze over

until we reached Gramphoo. There, where the road divided
I saw a thin boy in red flannel squat between two dhabas;

a black-eyed bean, slipped-in between two crags, he was so small
that I almost missed him, until he turned, gap-toothed, and shot me

with a toy gun. And a piece of me stopped then, though the bus moved on,
and the fat man beside me cracked open an apple with his thumb.

## Holy Cow

Wrapped inside a hawthorn nest on the bottom lip
of a mountain you find me waiting and shaking

and still holding my apple as I look up,
see the bruised peak rip open clouds, and spill

the monsoon rains all over again. Chuckling at my crown
of thorns, rain slopping down my face, you clack with the toads

as you untangle me. Your lips are older than the earth;
your hand is worn raw as you take me

over rocks, sloshing in flooded gullies and stumbling
through trees to a cowshed that smells hot, dark, wet.

You lead me inside, where it is still, except for the cow's tail swaying,
and your dark black braid swinging, and the steam rising up

and up, as I try to memorise the shape of my left foot
on a rock slab, the white of my apple core in the mud,

which bubbles and breathes as I crouch beside you
and your black eyed honey-skinned beast; she blinks and shivers too

when you touch her. Squatting, you lay your flat palms
on her stretched stomach, rest your cheek on her soft flank,

murmur into her velvet skin. And I think you will drink her then,
as the rain drinks up all sound, and you and me and the cow, we melt

into the darkness until we are utterly silent
except for our swallowing.

**Momos and Tea**

Afterwards, breaking through the skin of a 30 watt beam,
we walked out and into the middle depths of night

and stumbling across a ditch or a creek or a child,
we ducked into the Whispering Willow Café at the edge of Old Kaza

where a group of bug eyed men and three Israeli tourists
talked in low voices, a dim light humming, then blinking out.

When the waiter lit the candle, he glowed up good and bright;
his face utterly smooth, his eyes creaking a little as they met mine

and glancing up I saw that I was alone inside a dream box
with padded walls and ceiling like the mattress of our bed.

The waiter was very sorry: there was nothing he could give us
except momos and tea, which we ate and drank quickly,

listening to the small sounds of our sipping, before stripping
back the dusty notes, peeling ourselves apart

and slipping back into the darkness that hung there between us,
stumbling on and on through the night.

**Childish Things**

Spreading jam
on white buttered bread
I think of you

your silver-tipped lashes
your long-legged wrists
and how you liked

childish things
like stuffed koala bears
jam without the pips

and how you liked
to call me girl
and me to call you boy

and how you didn't want
a woman anyway
but a small slip of a thing

who would only eat
small sips of things
like tomato soup

or jam on toast
and how you liked
to see me laugh like a girl

and cry like a girl
and beg you please
I'm small, I'm clean.

**The Yard**

Afterwards, I move to a one-bed
with a yard: its ratty paving
cluttered with chipped pots

and moss-lined like your stubble;
the broken trellis reminds me
of my fractured elbow that time.

In the flowerbed I dig up tulip bulbs
and think they won't stop;
dream of them at night bubbling up

and down like garden peas in a pan.
I picture babies or your bald head
when we shaved it one spring.

The last tenants left six plastic chairs,
stacked. I put them out on the street
with a polite notice: Help yourself,

but no one does. I plant chopsticks
in the flowerbed – rude fingers
to stop the cats from crapping.

I haven't done any laundry for weeks
but I string a washing line anyway,
hang tea lights along it

so that at night, it's as if someone
is still watching me as I stretch out
on the cold, hard paving slabs.

**November**

I'm not entirely alone. The matron
sails back and forth through the fog
like a warship. I squint, try to read
the name on her file. Other than that

nothing happens, except rain,
which hangs from the trees
like an experiment. Every night
at eight, someone turns out the light

and they sharpen their pencils.
I heard somebody calling once,
and I don't know, perhaps a dog,
barking. It sounded far off.

Some days, I plan to break out,
but they say the walls are solid
bone reinforced with white paper.
Besides, I've seen their binoculars.

Instead, I curl up like a nut.
Yesterday, I found if I drop things
they make a noise but never break.
Later, I'll drop myself from the ceiling.

**Clam**

The beach at night is my body.
You taught me this,
and how goose barnacles
will slit your wrists
if you're not careful.

Tonight I'm fused with clams.
They stick upright like my sister's
fingernails or bunches of car keys
and when I try to run away from myself
they slice the soles of my bare blue feet.

I've never seen so much water:
it sluices through my bones
like your sperm, your spit,
its cold crawling up inside me
coming home in my chest.

You taught me about molluscs too;
how they have tongues for feet
kill dog whelks
by tethering them to rock
until they starve to death.

You always find me;
dragging me out of the sea again,
the water pours out of me again;
your boots snapping the clams
like children clapping.

**Footing**

The earth is soft
and I am sinking.
Beneath the mountain

the Chinese keep
engineered diseases
and black tanks.

Days pass without sign.
It is silent except
for water, aeroplanes.

Hours I do not sleep,
watch the submarines
slip by down there

like titanium eels.
Some days I smell
anthrax in the trees.

**Turn out the light**

And the heron-man
will be watching you sleep,
his long fingers will twist
your neck, peel your scalp
with his silver butter knife.
Slowly, he will draw out your dream
and crack it open on the side
of his blue china teacup.

Bonjour Julia, he will say,
greetings to your bonnet of bees -
Listen carefully, do what I say:
you must unbind your fire-sticks,
place your cheek on my paper -
and when you dream
you will write, and wake
wanting to uproot trees.